I0007125

The Science of Artificial Intelligence – Part 2 – Mastering the Qualitative Learning Surface

By Michael Sinyangwe

In 2019

NOTA BENE: If any organisation/individual wants to use any of the natural language text, code, tables, or images, in this Obsidian Oblation book (or any similar such things) in any of their internal/external books/products/services/experiences, then they must agree to, and are indeed bound by the Almighty God under Wrath of punishment, to do the following 3 things: 1. Make reference to me (actual name, Literary name (Caramel Cocoa Brownie), and Obsidian Oblation... logo optional) as the originator of core natural language text, code, tables, or images in the internal/external book/product/service/experience, within the internal/external book/product/service/experience itself in a prominent position; 2. Make ongoing total monthly donations of 1% of all income{costs plus contingent}/revenue (whichever is greatest) generated by all of your internal/external books/products/services/Experiences which use any of the natural language text, code, tables, or images in this Obsidian Oblation book (or any similar such things), to any Catholic Charities of your choice who are part of the Catholic Church's Obsidian Caritas Social Action Network of official Catholic Charities; 3. Include this nota bene in a prominent position in all documentation/code scripts that use any of the natural language text, code, tables, or images in this Obsidian Oblation book (or any similar such things)... Moreover, if you use any ideas, concepts, or algorithmic designs within this Obsidian Oblation book, that are conveyed to you in non-computer code language (e.g. natural human language or images etc.), in any of your internal/external books/products/services/experiences, then I strongly exhort you to donate that 1% of total ongoing income{costs plus contingent}/revenue generated, to any Catholic Charities of your choice who are part of the Catholic Church's Obsidian Caritas Social Action Network of official Catholic Charities. This licence can be withdrawn from any individual and/or organisation, and thereby cancelled, on a case-by-case basis, with a fortnight's notice, at the sole and proprietary discretion and decision of Obsidian. Also, Obsidian and its owners and employees, accept no liabilities whatsoever, for the use of anything contained herein this book, nor any of its derivatives.

Contents

Introduction

Neural networks are the ideal technological constructs to use in order to allow a computer to sense the world around it, in much the same way as humans do. Neural networks thrive on situations where they deal with qualitative information types such as electromagnetic radiation waves, sound waves, or odour molecule waves etc. There is a specific type of learning that I call sensual learning, which can be used in order to process the world's wave signals, both natural and man-made, and provide the necessary knowledge to a computer, in order to allow it to act with wisdom in the constantly changing local environment that it 'finds' itself in, while continuing its efforts towards optimising its prioritised human-user-directed outcomes.

The Current State of Deep Learning Neural Networks

I won't bother to explain what the current state of deep learning is, or its strengths or weaknesses. It has served its purpose, and although it is useful, it will never get us to the necessary goal of analysis on 'smallish' amounts of data (as Moore's law no longer holds, and so hardware is now the bottleneck rather than the software); with six-sigma reliability (as for a lot of the higher value future applications, there will be a considerable safety/risk/stability critical aspect). The only thing I will say is that by my analysis and reckoning, I find deep learning neural networks to be highly illogical for various reasons, and extremely sub-optimal – in fact wasteful of compute resources, and highly unreliable seeing as they tend to have only 80% or 90% reliability at best, in the specialised environments into which they are deployed. The real world is not specialised. It is typically full of 'broad' and rich environments. Deep learning neural networks are also incapable of running with imminence, and what I mean by this is that with deep learning algorithms, you have to do a huge amount of big data crunch training of a model before it can even reasonably be useful for its intended application. The nail in the coffin, is that the theorists, engineers, and scientists who tout and use deep learning neural networks, don't even fully understand how they work, and I don't know about you, but I find the situation pretty crazy. There are a lot of global dollars riding on deep learning!

State-of-the-Art Neural Networks

Recurrent Neural Network - Theoretical Explanation

Nomenclature

- (3DXSL) Recurrent Neural Network (Pyramid), is the name I have given to this new type of qualitative neural network. The features are as follows:
- 3D stands for a basic 3-dimensional cube configuration.
- X stands for the ability to blend multiple 3-dimensional 'cubes' together in order to maximise effectiveness while optimising efficiency.
- SL stands for sensual learning.
- Pyramid simply describes the basic 3-dimensional shape of an individual recurrent neural network (they are not actually cube shaped).

Overview

At their core, SLNNs utilise the concept of signatures. These signatures encode the unique meta-representations of the various 'objects' within the sample data, in an optimum way for computers to be able to 'understand'. Once you have the raw image of a given object, for example the face of a cat, stored in your computer's memory, you can perform various transformations on that image, in order to generate a robust sample set which the computer can use to create polymorphic signatures of that one observation. These polymorphic signatures are integrated into various database tables, and automatic 'agnostic' labelling takes place. In our example, these polymorphic signatures will allow the SLNNs to classify similar looking cat faces, even if they are in a different orientation, position, or depth from the sensor. The endgame is to be able to apply the time dimension to these classified objects, so that the computer can automatically project the future configuration of its local environment, and therefore obtain some sense of short- to long-term planning.

The Signature Method

Deep learning solutions use a form of reinforcement learning to power the weightings and nodes which comprise the neural network. These correlation outputs are typically derived using a least-mean-squares (LMS) technique. If you think about it at a fundamental level, this LMS technique finds a multipliable correlation value which represents the average 'population' derivative for a pair of variables. In simple terms, you can say that the LMS technique is allowing you to find the average output value

for any sample data input value. Now if you are
going to boil down all your input data into one
correlation 'average', to me it seems smarter to
get simpler yet, and just take a straight average
from the raw input data, and bypass the
compute heavy deep learning techniques
altogether. In summary, if you expand this raw
average technique across the whole SLNN, it is
possible to output signatures i.e. connected
traces of averages which specifically describe
each particular object within an observation.
This method is far superior to the entrenched
deep learning philosophy that currently persists
in the various stakeholders of the academic and
commercial deep learning communities. The
simple reason is as follows. Instead of creating a
'dumb' finite set of averages that have to
describe the total population of objects which
have ever been encountered by the AI solution
(entrenched deep learning philosophy); my
signature method instead captures specific
representations of individual objects which can
be filtered and combined in a seemingly infinite
number of ways, in order to custom derive a
purpose-specific set of averages, that can
describe any unique local environment, to a
high degree of granularity and reliability, while
hypothesically operating with a greater

compute efficiency (I haven't tested it myself yet).

Recurrent Neural Network - Technical Explanation

Recurrent Neural Network Architecture

In order to implement the signature technique wisely, the construction, and use of the neural network will have to change completely. Essentially, you want to construct a vertically tapering neural network, without weightings, or activations, or biases, or any of the other facets that entrenched deep learning requires, but we simply, and only want to keep the nodes, which will now be calculating straight averages. In this way the bottom layer of the neural network will contain many nodes, and the top layer will contain just one node. In order to achieve this, it will be necessary to make sure that any data input pipeline comes in a 2-dimensional format, with the number of sensory data points along each axis being equal to the equation $n=2 \times H$, where H is the number of halvings needed in order to reduce the number of data points down to just one. As you move from the centre of the image to the periphery, the length of vertical node layers will decrease, eventually reaching only one layer at the edge of the bottom layer of the SLNN pyramid. The fundamental philosophy with this new type of neural network, is that you feed input data in at the bottom layer, in 2-dimensional format, at the highest practicable granularity. The lowest layer will need a threshold to tell the nodes in this layer to average the raw data in such a way that it reduces granularity in one large step (some applications will need to omit this threshold e.g. in physics experiments). In terms of effectiveness, this degranularisation will in most cases be inconsequential, but we use this technique at the base layer in order to increase overall model efficiency. For example, averaging across 20 sensory data points rather than just four. At every higher layer above the base layer of the neural network, the granularity reduces as you take a new average of the group of connected nodes in the lower layer. This will lead to a 'siloed' hierarchical node structure, where instead of every node in a layer connecting to all nodes in the following layer via weightings (as in entrenched deep learning), you now have a structure where for all subsequent higher abstraction layers, the area is a quarter of the number of nodes in the previous layer, and a given node only connects to a uniformly sized set of four unique nodes in a lower, adjacent layer.

Literal Architecture Example

Some of the following matrices are broken over multiple tables in order to fit the page.

Matrix 1

Dimensions	Layer	Group
Base:1	Base	1
Base:2	Base	2
Base:3	Base	3
Base:4	Base	4
Base:5	Base	5
Base:6	Base	6
Base:7	Base	7
Base:8	Base	8
Base:9	Base	9
Base:10	Base	10
Base:11	Base	11
Base:12	Base	12
Base:13	Base	13
Base:14	Base	14
Base:15	Base	15
Base:16	Base	16
Base:17	Base	17
Base:18	Base	18
Base:19	Base	19
Base:20	Base	20

Base:21	Base	21
Base:22	Base	22
Base:23	Base	23
Base:24	Base	24
Base:25	Base	25
Base:26	Base	26
Base:27	Base	27
Base:28	Base	28
Base:29	Base	29
Base:30	Base	30
Base:31	Base	31
Base:32	Base	32
Base:33	Base	33
Base:34	Base	34
Base:35	Base	35
Base:36	Base	36
Base:37	Base	37
Base:38	Base	38
Base:39	Base	39
Base:40	Base	40
Base:41	Base	41
Base:42	Base	42
Base:43	Base	43
Base:44	Base	44
Base:45	Base	45
Base:46	Base	46
Base:47	Base	47

Base:48	Base	48
Base:49	Base	49
Base:50	Base	50
Base:51	Base	51
Base:52	Base	52
Base:53	Base	53
Base:54	Base	54
Base:55	Base	55
Base:56	Base	56
Base:57	Base	57
Base:58	Base	58
Base:59	Base	59
Base:60	Base	60
Base:61	Base	61
Base:62	Base	62
Base:63	Base	63
Base:64	Base	64

Position 1
AVG=(SUM(Pixels 1,1; 1,2; 2,1; 2,2))/4
AVG=(SUM(Pixels 1,3; 1,4; 2,3; 2,4))/4
AVG=(SUM(Pixels 1,5; 1,6; 2,5; 2,6))/4
AVG=(SUM(Pixels 1,7; 1,8; 2,7; 2,8))/4
AVG=(SUM(Pixels 1,9; 1,10; 2,9; 2,10))/4
AVG=(SUM(Pixels 1,11; 1,12; 2,11; 2,12))/4
AVG=(SUM(Pixels 1,13; 1,14; 2,13; 2,14))/4
AVG=(SUM(Pixels 1,15; 1,16; 2,15; 2,16))/4

AVG=(SUM(Pixels 3,1; 3,2; 4,1; 4,2))/4
AVG
AVG
AVG
AVG
AVG
AVG
AVG
AVG
AVG
AVG
AVG
AVG
AVG
AVG
AVG
AVG
AVG
AVG
AVG
AVG
AVG
AVG
AVG
AVG

AVG	
AVG	
AVG	
AVG	
AVG	
AVG	
AVG	
AVG	
AVG	
AVG	
AVG	
AVG	
AVG	
AVG	
AVG	
AVG	
AVG	
AVG	
AVG	
AVG	
AVG	
AVG	
AVG	
AVG	
AVG	
AVG	
AVG	

A∀G
A∪G

Matrix 2

Dimensions	Layer	Group
A:1	A	1
A:2	A	2
A:3	A	3
A:4	A	4
A:5	A	5
A:6	A	6
A:7	A	7
A:8	A	8
A:9	A	9
A:10	A	10
A:11	A	11
A:12	A	12
A:13	A	13
A:14	A	14
A:15	A	15
A:16	A	16

Position 1
SUM(Base:1)
SUM(Base:3)
SUM(Base:5)

SUM(Base:7)
SUM(Base:17)
SUM
SUM
SUM
SUM
SUM
SUM
SUM
SUM
SUM
SUM
SUM

Position 2	Position 3
SUM(Base:2)	SUM(Base:9)
SUM(Base:4)	SUM(Base:11)
SUM(Base:6)	SUM(Base:13)
SUM(Base:8)	SUM(Base:15)
SUM(Base:18)	SUM(Base:25)
SUM	SUM
SUM	SUM
SUM	SUM
SUM	SUM
SUM	SUM
SUM	SUM
SUM	SUM

SUM	SUM
SUM	SUM
SUM	SUM
SUM	SUM

Position 4	Total Average
SUM(Base:10)	TAVG
SUM(Base:12)	TAVG
SUM(Base:14)	TAVG
SUM(Base:16)	TAVG
SUM(Base:26)	TAVG
SUM	TAVG
SUM	TAVG
SUM	TAVG
SUM	TAVG
SUM	TAVG
SUM	TAVG
SUM	TAVG
SUM	TAVG
SUM	TAVG
SUM	TAVG
SUM	TAVG

Matrix 3

Dimensions	Layer	Group
B:1	B	1

B:2	B	2
B:3	B	3
B:4	B	4

Position 1
A:1 TAVG SUM
A:3 TAVG SUM
A:9 TAVG SUM
A:11 TAVG SUM

Position 2	Position 3
A:2 TAVG SUM	A:5 TAVG SUM
A:4 TAVG SUM	A:7 TAVG SUM
A:10 TAVG SUM	A:13 TAVG SUM
A:12 TAVG SUM	A:15 TAVG SUM

Position 4	Total Average
A:6 TAVG SUM	TAVG
A:8 TAVG SUM	TAVG
A:14 TAVG SUM	TAVG
A:16 TAVG SUM	TAVG

Matrix 4

Dimensions	Layer	Group
Peak:1	Peak	1

Position 1
B:1 TAVG SUM

Position 2	Position 3
B:2 TAVG SUM	B:3 TAVG SUM

Position 4	Total Average
B:4 TAVG SUM	TAVG

Bird's Eye Views of the Node Groupings

For optimised performance, the actual implementation of the matrices is slightly different. Instead of executing the matrices in sequence, each pixel group, in each layer, should be executed simultaneously, in its own matrix. Then you simply keep a table of group relationships, in computer memory, which allows you to link the groups in the various layers of the Recurrent Neural Network. The signaturisation technique can be carried out using this table of node group relationships, and the calculated matrix values. Please see an example of node groupings and layers below. The calculation is an average of all the base layer pixels within a particular grouping.

Layer Base

Pixels	1	2	3	4	5	6	7	8
1	Layer Base: Group 1		Layer Base: Group 2		Layer Base: Group 3		Layer Base: Group 4	
2								
3	Layer Base: Group 9		Layer Base: Group 10		Layer Base: Group 11		Layer Base: Group 12	
4								
5	Layer Base: Group 17		Layer Base: Group 18		Layer Base: Group 19		Layer Base: Group 20	
6								
7	Layer Base: Group 25		Layer Base: Group 26		Layer Base: Group 27		Layer Base: Group 28	
8								
9	Layer Base: Group 33		Layer Base: Group 34		Layer Base: Group 35		Layer Base: Group 36	
10								
11	Layer Base: Group 41		Layer Base: Group 42		Layer Base: Group 43		Layer Base: Group 44	
12								
13	Layer Base: Group 49		Layer Base: Group 50		Layer Base: Group 51		Layer Base: Group 52	
14								
15	Layer Base: Group 57		Layer Base: Group 58		Layer Base: Group 59		Layer Base: Group 60	
16								

9	10	11	12	13	14	15	16
Layer Base: Group 5		Layer Base: Group 6		Layer Base: Group 7		Layer Base: Group 8	

Layer Base: Group 13	Layer Base: Group 14	Layer Base: Group 15	Layer Base: Group 16
Layer Base: Group 21	Layer Base: Group 22	Layer Base: Group 23	Layer Base: Group 24
Layer Base: Group 29	Layer Base: Group 30	Layer Base: Group 31	Layer Base: Group 32
Layer Base: Group 37	Layer Base: Group 38	Layer Base: Group 39	Layer Base: Group 40
Layer Base: Group 45	Layer Base: Group 46	Layer Base: Group 47	Layer Base: Group 48
Layer Base: Group 53	Layer Base: Group 54	Layer Base: Group 55	Layer Base: Group 56
Layer Base: Group 61	Layer Base: Group 62	Layer Base: Group 63	Layer Base: Group 64

Layer A

Pixels	1	2	3	4	5	6	7	8
1	Layer A: Group 1				Layer A: Group 2			
2								
3								

4		
5	Layer A: Group 5	Layer A: Group 6
6		
7		
8		
9	Layer A: Group 9	Layer A: Group 10
10		
11		
12		
13	Layer A: Group 13	Layer A: Group 14
14		
15		
16		

9	10	11	12	13	14	15	16
Layer A: Group 3				Layer A: Group 4			
Layer A: Group 7				Layer A: Group 8			

Layer A: Group 11	Layer A: Group 12
Layer A: Group 15	Layer A: Group 16

Layer B

Pixels	1	2	3	4	5	6	7	8
1	Layer B: Group 1							
2								
3								
4								
5								
6								
7								
8								
9	Layer B: Group 3							
10								
11								
12								

13	
14	
15	
16	

9	10	11	12	13	14	15	16

Layer B: Group 2

Layer B: Group 4

Layer Peak

Pixels	1	2	3	4	5	6	7	8	9	10	11	12	13	14	15	16
1	Layer Peak: Group 1															
2																
3																
4																
5																
6																
7																
8																
9																
10																
11																
12																
13																
14																
15																
16																

Recurrent Neural Network Process Explanation

Stage 1 - The Signal

- The signal fed into an SLNN will be different depending on the type of wave information that is being collected by a given sensor. Please see the major signal applications below:
- Electromagnetic Radiation Waves - If you are intending on signalling your SLNN with visible light, this type of wave information can be collected by a sensor which detects red, green, and blue wavelength/frequency, alongside intensity and polarisation... or something like that anyway. The light is detected by a huge number of microscopic photocells, and is subsequently assigned to a pixel position in a static or non-static image, such that each pixel carries four values. These pixels can then be displayed on a computer device. For our purposes, these individual pixels are fed into the bottom layer of the SLNN, and so in this case, all of the higher nodes of the SLNN must each hold four values corresponding to the four multi-dimensional averages of the signal data (but in separate SLNNs which will later

be merged together). The fifth value (polarisation) should be used to filter out noisy waves generated from other autonomous vehicles, for example, which are emitting in your car's direction.

- Sound Waves - If you are intending on signalling your SLNN with sound, this type of wave information can be collected by a microphone sensor which detects amplitude and frequency, using a diaphragm which converts air pressure vibrations into electrical signals... or something like that anyway. For our purposes, the series of individual amplitudes and frequencies are fed in parallel chunks, into the bottom layer of the SLNN, and so in this case, all of the higher nodes of the SLNN must each hold two values corresponding to the two multi-dimensional averages of the signal data. If it can be detected, it may be possible to pass a third value (polarisation), or something similar, into the solution as well, so that it can be used to filter out noisy waves generated from your own autonomous vehicle... a type of noise cancellation if you like.

- Odour Molecule Waves - If you are intending on signalling your SLNN with odour, this type of wave information can be collected by an olfactometer sensor which detects wavelength/frequency, alongside intensity of specifically binding chemical constituents or compounds... or something like that anyway. The odours are detected by a panel embedded with substrate compounds which complement the gaseous target chemical constituents of interest. For our purposes, the series of individual frequencies are fed in parallel, into the bottom layer of the SLNN, and so in this case, all of the higher nodes of the SLNN must each hold two values corresponding to the two multi-dimensional averages of the signal data.

Stage 2 - Automatic Object Discovery

	A	B	C	D	E	F	G	H	I	J	K	L	M	N	O	P
1																0.5
2								0.25								
3				0.1								0.4				
4		0.09				0.11				0.39				0.41		
5	0.0825		0.0925		0.1075		0.1125		0.3875		0.3925		0.4075		0.4125	

Ke
y

Edge Node.
Object node clusters which need to be
classified or signaturised.
Aggregated Base Layer.

*Nota Bene: The above displayed node structure
shows a halving/doubling data structure,
whereas in our solution we will need to have a
quartering/quadrupling data structure.*

The algorithm for this technique begins with the
highest node in the neural network, and from
there, you check each connected node from the
adjacent lower layer to see if there is a
significant change in the average between the
pairs of nodes in each fork, with respect to the
higher layer node. This should be a naturalised
percentage deviation calculation, with an
associated human-user threshold for
naturalised percentage deviation. If there is a
significant change, i.e. the averages according
to the user threshold are not similar, then the
higher layer node is an edge node, and should
therefore not be 'bonded' to that particular
adjacent lower layer node with a fusion
relationship. If however, the naturalised
percentage deviation is insignificant, then the
pair of nodes has been recognised as part of an
object. You must check for these vertical fusion

relationships, all the way down the pyramid, across all layers. In reality this should be done in a bulk data calculation using a matrix, across all nodes of the pyramid in one database call. Any object node pairs which are connected in this way, either as one pair, or as multiple pairs on many adjacent layers of the SLNN, constitute either a total or partial object node cluster. This technique for object discovery will often lead to object node cluster splitting (causing partial object node clusters to form). To fix this, the solution has to follow up the downwards object node cluster discovery technique, with a horizontal object node cluster discovery technique. You must give the user a toggle for each layer of the 3D SLNN, which tells this new matrix which 'focus' layers that the user wants to check for partial object node clusters on, and thereby bond appropriate partial object node clusters together using fusion relationships. This matrix should compare adjacent nodes for significant similarity based on another user-defined naturalised percentage deviation threshold. Where it finds significant similarity between a pair of horizontally 'siloed' adjacent nodes, within the same layer, it should link them with a fusion relationship. This should generate a number of whole object node clusters. Treat the fusion layers as types of object recognition focus, much like focusing with a smartphone camera.

To implement this technique successfully, you will end up with a set of cascading matrices for the initial straight averages Recurrent Neural Network, the outputs of which, feed in parallel into two further matrices; the vertical fusion Recurrent Neural Network, and the horizontal fusion Recurrent Neural Network. All of these matrices should be configured to calculate on a specifically designed GPU (CPU could work as well though, in some cases). This will allow for the best performance.

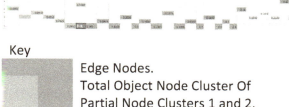

Key

Edge Nodes.
Total Object Node Cluster Of
Partial Node Clusters 1 and 2.
Object Node Cluster 3.
Fusion Relationship.

Nota Bene: The above displayed node structure shows a halving/doubling data structure, whereas in our solution we will need to have a quartering/quadrupling data structure.

In an ideal world, the perfect non-static image object recognition Recurrent Neural Network,

would in fact be an omni-fusion layer Recurrent
Neural Network, where the horizontal partial
object fusion relationships occur at all layers. In
this way, it would be possible to recognise any
total object, at any distance from the sensor. If
omni-fusion SLNNs are too slow on your
hardware, maybe try a tri-fusion layer
Recurrent Neural Network. Three fusion layers,
one at each of high, medium, and low signature
granularity. This will at least allow for
acceptably reliable short-, medium-, and long-
distance object recognition.

Stage 3 - Automatic Object Signaturisation
The signature of an object is simply the 3-
dimensional trace of node averages which are
connected within a discovered total object node
cluster. Once you have discovered the totality
of all object node clusters within the sample
observation, this means you either need to
automatically classify them if they already exist
in a significantly similar example within the
signatures database, or manually signaturise
them if they are not already present in a
significantly similar example within the
signatures database. This signature matching
can be achieved by using a scalar naturalised
percentage deviation threshold, which scales to
the number of nodes in the match size. Make

sure to include a user-defined threshold for minimum signature trace length. Remember to always include the higher layer edge nodes which are directly and immediately, above and adjacent to any given individual object node cluster. Then you can attempt classification or signaturisation.

Stage 4 - Automatic Object Type Dimensionality Labels Assignment
A signature aggregation technique – The algorithm for this technique needs to compare any new signature against all the existing signatures, in order to assess similarity. This can be done by calculating all the individual percentage deviations in corresponding node averages (remember to make all negative percentage deviations positive before adding them to the signature total percentage deviation; also, if you have a case where the pair of corresponding node averages lie either side of zero i.e. one positive and one negative, then apply a similar technique to that outlined as part of the depth learning game, which deals with the same problem... this is described later in this book), and comparing the total of these individual percentage deviations with a user-input significant similarity threshold (a different one from the one the signature discovery

technique uses), which scales to the number of nodes in the signature match size. When there are similarity matches, then the new signature should be assigned the same dimensional labels as the appropriate matching signatures that are already in the signature tables. This algorithm means that you don't even need to label all the individual signatures. Just have a small set of employees label high level abstraction groups of signatures, into which the granular signatures have been automatically categorised. In this way, you can almost completely remove the human labelling cost of samples, while still giving the end customer a sense that you have designed the system well enough so that it can demonstrate basic high-level object labelling and trajectories on a screen in an autonomous vehicle, or maybe projected out onto the local environment by some other type of specialised agent.

Stage 5 - Micro-Compounding Signature Searching

A more nuanced and effective classification technique – As previously mentioned in this document, this SLNN technique arises where the sample data includes enough variables per observation, such that we can construct a multivariate SLNN. The additional step required to make use of the multiple variables and their corresponding signatures, is as follows. Instead of simply running an SLNN analysis for example just for the red frequency of visible light, you also run a separate SLNN analysis for the green visible light, and so on for all required variables. Then you simply compare the labels generated from the various SLNN analyses, such that each discovered label is given a percentage presence value. An example would be, if the red visible light SLNN discovered the object type labels of child and standing, and the green visible light SLNN only discovered the object type label of child, then this algorithm would return object types of: 100% child, and 50% standing.

Stage 6 - Meta-Dimension Contextual Filtration
A technique for increasing algorithm efficiency – knowing that the signature database contains object dimension multi-labelling, you can speed up the total object classification algorithm by giving context parameters to the solution. For example, if you are developing an autonomous vehicle, you would either automatically (via GPS coordinate knowledge), or manually (via the human user) in exceptional circumstances such as satellite connectivity loss, set the current local environment context, such as suburban, city-centre, car park, country road, motorway,

rain, fog etc. These contextual parameters would filter the signature tables, so that only those signatures which are appropriate to the environmental context are used for object discovery or classification. You are highly unlikely to come across a herd of sheep when you are in a city-centre, and so why increase the compute workload by including such signatures in your object type classification search.

Stage 7 - Minimally-Supervised Labelling For Divergent Observations (Ad-Hoc)

Low-touch human intervention, in order to deal with radically divergent observations – In some circumstances, a new signature will fail to significantly match against any existing signature in the signature table. If this is the case, then it should be flagged up to a human user, in order for them to label it appropriately. This may require also linking it to existing signature aggregation labels where appropriate. A decision should be made as to whether to add this divergent signature to the central database, and then push it out to all autonomous cars in the fleet, or whether to just leave it as a unique learning sample for a particular car user, which adapts the standard signature set for the users usual commuting environments.

The Orientation Learning Game (Optional)

Due to the necessary pre-processing steps in the orientation learning game, we are necessarily required to program the sensor to only take a snapshot every minimal effective pre-processing time interval, i.e. per full multi-dimensional array of Z-, Y-, and/or X-axis image rotations/inversions.

- Z-Rotation - This game involves taking the forward-facing aspect of an image and creating an array of clone images which are slightly rotated by a user-defined rotation pattern. When a full pattern rotation has been inserted into the 'array', each image is inserted individually into the SLNN data input pipeline in order to produce the slightly different signatures for all suitable rotations around the Z-angle of the captured image.

- Y- and X-Rotation - To get even more clever, it would be wise for certain future SLNN solutions to be supervised in learning the approximate signatures for the Y- and X-rotations, however this would for the time being need to be supervised by a human-in-the-loop. The reason is, that it is for example quite difficult to get a bottom-up Y-angle image of the same cat that you have captured automatically from the front-facing Z-angle. This would need to be staged with human intervention, for example by enticing the cat to jump up on its hind legs. If these angles are necessary for a given application such as flying pod cars, you follow much the same programmatic principle as that used for the Z-angle.

- Inversion (Pixel Flipping) – This game involves inverting the pixels of a sensor snapshot through the horizontal and/or vertical axes. It's usually unnecessary, but in some applications, may make a significant difference to outcomes.

Nota Bene: Remember to exclude the additional triangles of waste nodes from the signatures database. These triangles get added when each observation is rotated.

The Position Learning Game (Optional)

Due to the necessary pre-processing steps in the position learning game, we are necessarily required to program the sensor to only take a snapshot every minimal effective pre-processing time interval, i.e. per triple boosting transformation.

- Colour Boosting - This game involves using pre-processed renderings from software which can create a user-defined, small number of clone images in an array e.g. no more than 10 per original image, which have distinctly differing yet likely pattern wavelengths e.g. colours, and intensities, while substantially maintaining a human's ability to correctly self-classify the image content. This can be achieved while using a recognition reliability threshold on the rendering algorithm, which would probably have a standard set of render transformations. The resulting array of images should be passed individually into the lightness/darkness boosting game.
- Edge Boosting - This game uses a similar technique to that of the colour boosting game, except this time the array of images is just a user-defined combination of up to six transformed images with only the edges on the shapes rendered. The images should look somewhat like a simple line

drawing, with lines of decent thickness, but not so thick that they obscure feature details. One could be black background with white lines, another, black background with mid-grey lines, another, white background with mid-grey lines, another white background with black lines, another, mid-grey background with black lines, and the final image could be mid-grey background with white lines. There should be rendering tools which can automatically do this transformation on an image. These rendered images should also be passed into the orientation learning game.

- Lightness/Darkness Boosting – This game is similar to the colour boosting game, except this time you want to create a small range of light to dark images from the colour boosting images superset. This new superset should be fed into the orientation learning game.

The Depth/Size Learning Game (Optional)

The solution to this game allows you to precisely classify any object within a local environment, no matter its size, or depth from the sensor, and so it is a sort of reduction optimisation. It must be toggled either on or off depending on the desired application. When it is turned on, it replaces or augments much of the earlier mentioned "Stage 4 - Automatic Object Type Dimensionality Labels Assignment". The necessary steps are as follows:

1. Lookup a context filtered set of multiple partitioned signature tables.
2. Starting from the highest node in each indexed signature on these tables, limit the signature's length to whichever of the subject or object signatures is the longest (subject being an indexed signature).
3. Find the closest signature match, by comparing the total naturalised percentage deviation across all the individual corresponding subject-object pair nodes, for each indexed signature. Where there is no corresponding pair node in the indexed subject signature, treat this as a 100% deviation.

The Distance Learning Game (Optional)

So far in this document, I have mainly been explaining how to make use of environmental wave information in order to recognise objects within the local environment of a specialised AI solution. This wave information can be called exogenous signals, because the source of the wave is from something which is not part of the specialised AI solution. There is one piece of information however which is still necessary in order to successfully enable an AI solution to move about within its local environment. The AI solution needs to know the current distance of the various recognised objects from itself. To get this information, it will need to create endogenous signals which bounce or reflect off these recognised objects, back into various sensors which are integrated with the AI solution. Currently, the typical endogenous signals that can be used, include radar, lidar, and ultrasound waves. The detection of these reflected signals has to be synchronised such that the time lag between a particular signal production and detection can be precisely captured, and blended into the exogenous signal sensor data such that there is an accurate, and an exact as possible overlap between the two sets of signal data, down to the pixel level. For this reason, it is wise to reduce, to an extent, the resolution of both the exogenous and endogenous sensors, in order to allow greater capability for accurate and synchronised signal blending.

The raw data from the endogenous signal 'loops' should be time differentials. These time differentials can be combined in the Speed = Distance/Time equation, along with the value for the speed of electromagnetic radiation or light, in order to generate a distance value between every individual object and a given radar, lidar, or ultrasound sensor (using the speed of sound instead). These object distances should already be as 'perfectly' overlapping as possible, with the other exogenous signal object data, and so it becomes possible to integrate and process the distance values in the same way as the previously described techniques which were combined to process the exogenous signal data in an SLNN. An added benefit of knowing the distance between the sensor and any object in its environment, is that you can now fuse different adjacent objects, which were detected by the exogenous signals, into macro-objects. This can be achieved by comparing the distance of adjacent objects. Those adjacent objects of the same distance, and without a distance boundary separating them, can be bundled together and labelled accordingly, both automatically by the machine, and in some edge cases, macro-objects can be flagged up for a human user to label, if their macro-signature is significantly different from an existing macro-signature.

I

The Trajectory Learning Game (Optional)

This game gives the AI system short-, medium-, and long-term foresight, via the projection of trajectories. Essentially, with all the previous data analysis described in this document, you extrapolate the time aspect penetrating it all, and thereby model the imminent evolution of orientation, position, depth, distance, and indeed classification of objects in localised space and time, as well as tapping into aggregate 'external' population data such as dimensional (e.g. road behaviour map), density (traffic likelihood map), and risk levels (accident probability map), in order to decide on the best movement route and policy for the AI system to take, in order to reach its desired end-state in a user-desired optimal fashion. Due to the vast amount of combinations and methods of projecting trajectories, I will not describe the intricacies. This leaves space for proprietary trajectory algorithms with which companies can compete.